15 BASIC BIBLICAL KEYS TO POVERTY

15 BASIC BIBLICAL KEYS TO POVERTY

If you know what causes it, you can avoid it.

Anthony Adefarakan

GLOEM, CANADA

Dedication

I dedicate this book to God Almighty for His goodness and faithfulness in making His Word available to me. All glory to His Holy Name.

Also to everyone facing one financial challenge or the other, I stand with you all and decree that you are coming out stronger in Jesus' Name.

Acknowledgement

I sincerely acknowledge my Eternal Father, Who alone is the Source of all wisdom. He is the Author and Finisher of my faith and it is of His fullness that the contents of this book have been drawn.

Also, I want to profoundly appreciate my dear parents – Prince and Mrs. Timothy Adefarakan – for bringing me up in the way of the Lord and for instilling righteousness consciousness in me. The wonderful education foundation I was given, coupled with their constant encouragement has empowered me to reach heights that were once beyond my imagination.

My most special appreciation goes to my sweetheart, Abisolami; without her help and support I would never have enjoyed the conducive atmosphere needed to publish this book. I appreciate your love, encouragement, and the support you give at all times. Thank you so much. I love you my Baby!

And to all my mentors in Ministry, I appreciate you all. Your investments in my life are not in vain. May the Lord reward you all in Jesus' Name.

Introduction

Several teachings abound in the Body of Christ when it comes to the subject of Prosperity, and there is actually nothing wrong with that; after all, it's the will of God for His children to prosper.

Psalm 35:27 says *"Let them shout for joy, and be glad, that favour my righteous cause: yea, let them say continually, Let the Lord be magnified, which hath pleasure in the prosperity of his servant."* And 3 John 2 also says *"Beloved, I wish above all things that thou mayest prosper and be in health, even as thy soul prospereth."*

However, the Lord recently laid it on my heart to also study steps to Poverty as revealed in His Word; the discovery of which will accomplish at least four (4) things:

15 BASIC BIBLICAL KEYS TO POVERTY

1. To prevent people from becoming poor- by avoiding the causes of poverty.

2. To explain to people why they are poor- by comparing their lives with the causes of poverty.

3. To help the poor overcome their poverty- by stepping out of the causes of poverty
and
4. To help those who have chosen to be poor know what to do in order to attract poverty- by engaging in the causes of poverty. After all, Jesus said the poor you will always have among you (Matthew 26:11).

So whichever category you belong, this is relevant; and I will like to implore you to pay rapt attention as we explore this important subject: **15 Basic Biblical Keys to Poverty!**

I pray as you read on, God's grace to apply this knowledge will rest upon you in Jesus' Name.

Anthony Adefarakan.

ANTHONY ADEFARAKAN

Key #1

Uncontrolled Sleep

Proverbs 6:9-11 (AMP) says:
"How long will you sleep, O Sluggard? When will you arise out of your sleep? Yet a little sleep, a little slumber, a little folding of the hands to lie down and sleep - So will your poverty come like a robber or one who travels (with slowly but surely approaching steps) and your want like an armed man (making you helpless)."

Sleep is good but uncontrolled sleep is a disaster. Sleeping when one should be working is a clear and official invitation to poverty and shame. Proverbs 10:5 (NLT) says sleeping away the hour of opportunity brings shame; and Proverbs 23:21 says too much sleep clothes a person with rags (typical of poverty).

Sleep should be earned after work; it's primarily designed to calm our nerves, relax our muscles, rejuvenate our bodies and mind thereby getting them ready for another task. You don't just sleep because there is nothing else to do. That's what invites poverty.

If you are unemployed or physically incapacitated to work, sleeping is not the way out. Instead of just lying down, engage your mind in meditation, read books, pray, encourage someone, go on the internet and carry out productive research, write books, paint pictures, volunteer your services somewhere - by all means, make sure you are adding value. This way, you will keep poverty away from your life.

Look at your life now; are you guilty of this poverty inviter? You know what? Even if you are rich today, if you keep breaking this law (sleeping uncontrollably), I can assure you by the Word of the Lord, you will eventually come to poverty because the scriptures cannot be broken.

Always remember this, there is a time to sleep and there is a time to refrain from sleeping. Proverbs 20:13 (NLT) says "If you love sleep, you will END in poverty. Keep your eyes open, and there will be plenty to eat!" (Emphasis mine). Start controlling your sleep!!!

Key #2

Oppressing the Poor

Proverbs 22:16 (NIV) says:
"One who oppresses the poor to increase his wealth...come to poverty."

How clear and concise God's Word can be!

To oppress the poor is to burden them with cruel or unjust impositions or restraints; subject them to a burdensome or harsh exercise of authority or power. It also means to treat them cruelly, or to prevent them from having the same opportunities, freedom, and benefits as others. And unfortunately, these abound all around us today.

The Word of God has a lot to say about the consequences of such. For instance, Psalm 12:5 says God arises for the oppression of the poor and according to Psalm 72:4, He breaks the oppressor in pieces.

Beware of the following:
I. Willfully refusing to pay the wages of your workers on time is oppression (Deuteronomy 24:14-15).

II. Using your workers' salary to do business in order to accumulate some interest is oppression.

III. Taking bribes to pervert justice for the poor is oppression.

IV. Collecting money from the poor before giving them what is rightfully theirs or not rendering the services they pay for is oppression.

V. Charging interests when you lend to the poor is oppression (Exodus 22:25).

VI. Stealing from the poor to increase your possessions or collecting offerings and tithes from them for personal gains is oppression.

VII. Buying from the poor and willfully refusing to pay them the agreed amount or not even paying them on time is oppression.

Anything you do against the poor in order to get some profits or financial benefits for yourself qualifies as OPPRESSING THE POOR TO INCREASE YOUR RICHES. And if you don't repent today with plans to urgently restitute, you shall soon become poor (that's if you are not already poor). The Lord has spoken!

Key #3

Showering Gifts on the Rich

Proverbs 16:22 (NLT) says:
"A person who gets ahead...by showering gifts on the rich will end in poverty."

How good it is to discover that many people ended up in poverty just because they kept giving to the rich! Honestly if not that it is written in God's Word, I would have argued it out on the basis of "giving is giving, whether to the poor or to the rich"; but God's Word is forever settled in Heaven, and He says giving to the rich in order to increase your riches (or get ahead) will qualify you for poverty.

The rich has been described as one who has wealth or great possessions; abundantly supplied with resources, means, or funds; wealthy.

Showering gifts on anyone who fits this description (especially in order to increase your own chances of becoming rich) will lead to poverty, but showering gifts on the poor (who have no means of ever repaying you) is what keeps poverty out of your life - Proverbs 19:17 (TM).

Doesn't make sense, right? Yeah, but it sure makes faith and moreover that's how God wants it. So if I were you, I would just fall in line and begin to focus my giving on those really in need. That's where the blessings are!

There are several poor orphans, widows, farmers and even local workers in the third world nations who are practically struggling to survive on a daily basis. They wake up not knowing where their breakfast is coming from and they most times go to bed on empty stomachs. These are the people God wants us to focus our giving on, not those who are so rich that they no longer know what to do with their wealth other than to waste it. Do what the Word of God says regardless of what you think or feel, there is a blessing for doing so. And in this case, the blessing is in the fact that you will escape poverty.

Key #4

Idle Chatter

Proverbs 14:23 (NIRV) says:
"All hard work pays off. But if all you do is talk, you will be poor".

This is one key to becoming poor that has been considered of little or no importance by many, yet it has dealt greatly with its victims. The King James Version calls it idle chatter.
This verse of the Bible implies that every time a person chooses to replace working with idle talks, useless gists, gossiping, unproductive chatting, pointless discussions etc, POVERTY IS THE END RESULT.

I have personally seen people in offices chatting and discussing sports, movies, among other irrelevant things as early as 8:00am-10:00am while their colleagues were busy getting things done for the day. These are the kind of people who usually finish up their salaries ever before they are paid. They are always in need.

I have also observed some able-bodied men who gather at newspaper stands as early as 7:00am-10:00am, shouting and arguing about politics, sports etc while others are busy somewhere making money. Such is a clear invitation to poverty.

Chatting is not bad, discussing sports and movies are not sinful, HOWEVER IF THAT IS ALL YOU DO WITH YOUR TIME, ACCORDING TO THE WORD OF GOD, YOU SHALL BE POOR. This also includes talking about your intentions and plans without engaging in the necessary labour to achieve them. That is, all you say is "I will do this, I plan doing that" without taking the necessary steps. Poverty is what eventually shows up.

Always remember this: There is a time to talk

and there is a time to keep quiet. Discern these times in your own life and all will be well. Now, it's time to get busy!

Key #5

Withholding more than is Right

Proverbs 11:24 (NKJV) says:
"There is one who scatters, yet increases more; And there is one who withholds more than is right, But it leads to poverty."

ESV Rendition:
"One gives freely, yet grows all the richer; another withholds what he should give, and only suffers want."

NCV Rendition:
"Some people give much but get back even more. Others don't give what they should and end up poor."

NIRV Rendition:
"Some give freely but get even richer. Others

don't give what they should but get even poorer."

When it comes to money, it has been said that a man's wealth is not dependent on how much he makes but how much he keeps. And this is very true.

It's good to save; it's good to be prudent; and it's good to keep money for different things. These are all good practices that can increase one's wealth, at least from the financial experts' perspectives.

However, the Word of God says "WITHHOLDING MORE THAN IS RIGHT" will lead one to poverty.

How?
1. Keeping back your tithe under the guise of trying to save will eventually qualify you for poverty.
2. Holding back your offerings and seeds will open the door to poverty.
3. Holding back your workers' wages will end you

up in poverty.

4. Closing your ears to the cries of the poor around you (by not blessing them) under the guise of trying to conserve money will lead to poverty.

5. Not being charitable at all because of tight financial schedules and plans is a road that leads to poverty.

It is good to "withhold" - that is being prudent BUT it is bad to "withhold more than is right" - that is being stingy.

According to ESV, NIRV and NCV as rendered above, WITHHOLDING WHAT YOU SHOULD GIVE WILL ATTRACT POVERTY TO YOUR LIFE.

The Bible says God ministers seed to the sower and bread to the eater (Isaiah 55:10 KJV; 2 Corinthians 9:10 KJV). That means there are certain provisions that God allows to come your way because He actually wants you to pass them on to where they are meant to go and to those who need them. Those are seeds which include your tithes and offerings, alms, gifts to both your biological and spiritual parents, gifts to the underprivileged ones, support for Gospel causes like evangelistic crusades and missions all over the world, disaster relief packages among other charitable donations. [Read Exodus 20:12, Galatians 6:6, Galatians 6:10, 1 Timothy 5:17, Matthew 6:3-4 and 2 Corinthians 9:9].

Withholding what should go to these covenant channels as God (the Provider) expects is what attracts poverty because He will simply stop sending them through you.

There was a time in my local church when contributions were being made towards an upcoming evangelistic outreach and we were to make certain financial commitments towards it. I didn't have mine handy at the moment; but before the due date, a man (who was not even a Christian) blessed me with that same amount I needed to contribute without asking him for it. Right there I knew God had just ministered seed for me to sow; so I simply dropped everything towards the success of the crusade and praised God for the opportunity.

Now, that provision didn't come to me as 'bread to the eater' so it would been very wrong of me to spend it on my needs. The God Who ministers seed to the sower also ministers 'bread' for your consumption; when He brings the 'bread' you are very much at liberty to withhold it for your own use.

Learn to differentiate between what you should keep and what you should give and let your budget reflect that. That is how to escape the peril of withholding more than is right. May the Lord bless your finances.

Key #6

Laziness

Proverbs 10:4 (NLT) says:
"Lazy people are soon poor; hard workers get rich."

Laziness is the quality of being unwilling to work or use energy; idleness.
Lazy people are averse or disinclined to work, activity, or exertion; they are indolent. And according to the Authorized King James Version, a lazy person is one 'that dealeth with a slack hand.'

If someone is lazy, they do not want to work or make any effort to do anything; and this cuts across all fields of human endeavour.
For instance, there can be lazy doctors, lazy engineers, lazy nurses, lazy teachers, lazy husbands, lazy wives, lazy children, lazy students, lazy apprentices,

15 BASIC BIBLICAL KEYS TO POVERTY

lazy businessmen, and even lazy men of God who rush to the pulpit to preach dead sermons instead of taking enough time to prepare fresh messages with which to feed God's flock.

This list also includes lazy Christians who only quote whatever they hear from their Pastors, friends and the internet without spending quality time researching answers from the Bible which always lies unattended to by their bedsides.

Now, there is this other dimension of laziness that I saw in the Bible; it's in Proverbs 12: 27. The New King James Version renders it this way: *"The lazy man does not roast what he took in hunting, But diligence is man's precious possession."*

You know what that means? It means a lazy person may actually hunt for opportunities, but they will never process anyone they come across; and as a result, they will not benefit from them. That simply suggests that lazy bones experience wasted efforts as a lifestyle. They never follow through on anything.

At this point, I believe even the blind should

have been able to see that poverty is actually spiritual. It may manifest in physical forms but its roots are not really physical. There are so many things we take for granted that attract poverty into our lives.

This is a sure prophecy for all lazy bones according to the Word of the Lord — UNLESS YOU REPENT, YOU SHALL SOON BE POOR!
The following scriptural verses affirm this;
Proverbs 13:4 NIV - *"A sluggard's appetite is never filled, but the desires of the diligent are fully satisfied."*

Proverbs 20:4 ISV – *"A lazy person doesn't plow in the proper season; he looks for a harvest, but there is nothing."*

Proverbs 19:15 CEV – *"If you are lazy and sleep your time away, you will starve."*

Key #7

Making Yourself Rich

Proverbs 13:7a (NKJV) says:
"There is one who makes himself rich, yet has nothing..."

The Aramaic Bible in Plain English renders it this way:
"There are those who enrich themselves and have nothing..."

Enriching yourself will lead to obsession and you will never have enough that way. Ecclesiastes 5:10 (NIV) confirms this; "Whoever loves money never has enough; whoever loves wealth is never satisfied with their income..."

One major characteristic of people who fall into this category is greed. When greed is at work, you simply become blind to other people's needs while amassing wealth and possessions for selfish reasons. Read the Parable Jesus gave in Luke 12:14-21 (NLT) to explain this point:

"Jesus replied... "Beware! Guard against every kind of greed. Life is not measured by how much you own."

Then he told them a story: "A rich man had a fertile farm that produced fine crops. He said to himself, 'What should I do? I don't have room for all my crops.' Then he said, 'I know! I'll tear down my barns and build bigger ones. Then I'll have room enough to store all my wheat and other goods. And I'll sit back and say to myself, "My friend, you have enough stored away for years to come. Now take it easy! Eat, drink, and be merry!"'

"But God said to him, 'You fool! You will die this very night. Then who will get everything you worked for?'

"Yes, a person is a fool to store up earthly wealth but not have a rich relationship with God."

If all you think about is how to keep enriching yourself without giving any thought to enriching

others, the Word of God says you will end up with nothing, and that is typical of being poor.
Beware of this Biblical key to poverty.

Key #8

Disdaining Correction

Proverbs 13:18a (NKJV) says:
"Poverty and shame will come to him who disdains correction..."

To despise or treat wise correction with contempt is an open invitation to poverty and her bosom friend, shame. If you feel you are above correction or you are used to saying "I know what I am doing, no one should correct me", sooner or later poverty is going to find her way to your house.

For example, you decided to go into business and you started putting all the logistics in place but did not prepare any business plan. A very good friend of yours who is also vast in matters relating to business decided to point out the fact that you needed a business plan in place before embarking on the project. Well, you heard him but didn't take any of his corrections. So you just kept embarking on projects without writing down your business plans; according to the Word of God, a time is coming when you will attract a crushing dimension of poverty as you begin to lose money repeatedly.

Every time you disdain spiritual or wise correction or counsel, you attract poverty and shame. Proverbs 29:1 NLT says: *"If you get more stubborn every time you are corrected, one day you will be crushed and never recover."* This is a Biblical key to poverty.

Key #9

Loving Pleasure

Proverbs 21:17 (NKJV) says
"He who loves pleasure will be a poor man; He who loves wine and oil will not be rich."

If your philosophy of life is wrapped up in having fun and just enjoying luxuries, partying all day and feasting away your income, you are a lover of pleasure, and 1 Timothy 5:6 NET says *"...the one who lives for pleasure is dead even while she lives."*

If you have no plan to undergo temporary inconvenience in order to save for your future, no specific plans for investment, no prudent living and careful spending, then you are likely to fulfill this Prophecy of Poverty according to the text above.

15 BASIC BIBLICAL KEYS TO POVERTY

Pleasure isn't bad in itself, the love of it is what brings about the siege of poverty into a person's life. Don't just earn to spend. You are still living in a rented apartment but whenever you get paid, all you spend your money on are luxurious cars, vacations in choicest locations around the world, dinner parties etc. That's not the pathway to wealth.

Good News Translation renders that Proverbs 21:17 this way:

"Indulging in luxuries, wine, and rich food will never make you wealthy."

Invest in your future and plan to escape poverty by enduring temporal inconveniences in order to reach your financial goals. That's the principle of delayed gratification.
Don't be a lover of pleasure.

Key #10

Borrowing

Proverbs 22:7 (GNT) says:
"Poor people are slaves of the rich. Borrow money and you are the lender's slave."

You may not appreciate this Scripture until you check up the word 'slave' in the dictionary. One dictionary describes a slave as someone who is the property of another person and has to work for that person. It further describes a slave as someone who is completely under the control of another person or of a powerful influence.

Whether you believe it or not, as a borrower you are not free from your lender (bank or person). And as long as this continues, your poverty remains because the spiritual still controls the physical.

15 BASIC BIBLICAL KEYS TO POVERTY

Do this test, calculate all you are owing to people and banks and subtract the total from the money you can confidently call your own. The answer will tell you your true state. No borrower boasts of financial freedom. Never!

Now, I quite understand there are extreme circumstances when you will have to borrow – maybe for health reasons, educational purposes, family emergencies, time-bound investment opportunities etc; yes I know borrowing may be the only way out at such times. But the point I'm making is this, don't make it a lifestyle. If you are indebted in anyway, your urgent goal should be how to make repayment. You are not supposed to be boasting and living large on borrowed funds. That's what I call 'living a borrowed life' and that's where the slavery comes in. You will keep answering to your lender as long as you are still in possession of their fund.

One more thought on borrowing; when you are in debt, you can't have the liberty of giving freely. You may want to make certain donations, but because of your loans, you may have constraints and not be able to go on with it.

Are you in any form of debt now? Work out a concrete modality to clear them off and start afresh as a free man.

Key #11

Drunkenness/Gluttony

Proverbs 23:21 (GNT) says:
"Drunkards and gluttons will be reduced to poverty. If all you do is eat and sleep, you will soon be wearing rags."

Simply put, drunkenness implies getting drunk while gluttony implies excessive eating and drinking. If you know anyone who doesn't know when to say 'ENOUGH' or 'STOP' when it comes to eating and drinking, you have the authority of the Scripture to tell them to get ready for poverty. It's a law. Poverty must surely visit them (unless they repent). The Scriptures cannot be broken.

Take a closer look at the first part of that text (Proverbs 23: 21). It says *'Drunkards and gluttons will be reduced to poverty...*"

You know what that means? It means even if you are very rich today, but you keep indulging in excessive drinking and eating, you will be REDUCED to poverty, and that's not the kind of position you want to find yourself in. This is a Biblical key to poverty.

Key #12

Hasty Plans

Proverbs 21:5 (NKJV) says:
"The plans of the diligent lead surely to plenty, But those of everyone who is hasty, surely to poverty."

(GWT) says:
"The plans of a hard-working person lead to prosperity, but everyone who is [always] in a hurry ends up in poverty."

Hasty plans imply acting too quickly without thinking carefully. For instance, not all good looking investments are actually profitable.
Now, many of us have acted too quickly by getting involved in some good looking but bad investments at one time or the other and some of us have

even lost good money in the process. Such will not necessarily lead to poverty.

But according to God's Word Translation (GWT) as quoted above, doing this always- that is, always acting too quickly (hastily) in matters relating to our finances will eventually result in poverty. Someone has said: "Better to be slow and sure, than to be fast and fail". This is very true. Isaiah 28:16 (NKJV) says "...Whoever believes will not act hastily" - so hasty plans indicate unbelief. And Proverbs 11:14 says in the multitude of counsellors there is safety - which implies seeking good counsels and engaging in careful researches in matters relating to our finances can bring about financial safety. Hasty and careless (financial) plans will lead to poverty.

Look at what Proverbs 19:2 ERV says:
"Being excited about something is *not enough. You must also know what you are doing. Don't rush into something, or you might do it wrong."*

And also Proverbs 21:5 TPT;

*"Brilliant ideas pay off and bring you prosperity,
but making hasty, impatient decisions
will only lead to financial loss."*
Beware of this Biblical key to poverty!

Key #13

Following Frivolity

Proverbs 28:19 (NKJV) says:
"He who tills his land will have plenty of bread, But he who follows frivolity will have poverty enough!"

GNT says:
"A hard-working farmer has plenty to eat. People who waste time will always be poor."

Question:
What does it mean to follow frivolity?

Answer:
According to the Cambridge Dictionary, frivolity simply implies behaviour that is silly and

not serious, or things that are silly and not important.

To follow frivolity therefore is to keep wasting time on unimportant things; showing lack of seriousness and behaving as if time doesn't matter. Living like this sucks up the time that should have been spent on important profitable things and as a result makes one leave important things unattended.

Question:
How does that lead to poverty?

Answer:
Living like that is what the Bible says attracts poverty because most opportunities in life are tied to time. So, the one who wastes time on frivolities as a lifestyle will not be able to seize opportunities when they come knocking.

Having this repeated is what eventually culminates in poverty. No one who doesn't have respect for time will ever taste lasting wealth. Time wasters always end up poor. Don't be a Time-Waster!

ANTHONY ADEFARAKAN

Key #14

Hastening after Riches

Proverbs 28:22 (NKJV) says:
"A man with an evil eye hastens after riches, And does not consider that poverty will come upon him."

GNT says:
"Selfish people are in such a hurry to get rich that they do not know when poverty is about to strike."

Question:
How would you describe this as a factor responsible for poverty?

Answer:
When you become so concerned about making money that you literally forget to take certain pre-

cautions in order to prevent losses; you are beginning to look like the fellow in our text as rendered by the Good News Translation.

Just imagine someone loading up their bank accounts with money without checking the integrity of the financial institutions they are with. Now, after depositing millions upon millions in those accounts, news now comes out that the bank accounts are fake and that the funds are untraceable because they do not actually exist. Could you imagine the heartache that will visit such fellow? Such is the experience of people who hasten after riches and get caught up in poverty.

Key #15

Dwelling in Famine

Genesis 45:10-11 (NKJV) says:
"You shall dwell in the land of Goshen, and you shall be near to me, you and your children, your children's children, your flocks and your herds, and all that you have. There I will provide for you, lest you and your household, and all that you have, come to poverty; for there are still five years of famine."

Question:

What is the correlation between famine and poverty?

Answer:

An online dictionary has described famine as extreme and general scarcity of food, as in a country or a large geographical area. Any extreme and general scarcity. Extreme hunger; starvation.

Now, summarizing this in one word, we can safely say famine means lack. As for the correlation between famine and poverty, if famine means lack, then it connotes poverty.

During famine, the rain needed for crops to grow and produce food for people does not fall and as a result, food scarcity sets in. And because people will do anything in order to eat, they begin to sell their possessions so as to buy the little food available or they even go to other places in search of food which was the case of Joseph's brothers who came to Egypt to buy some food as directed by their father, Jacob.

It is worthy of note that famine is in a different category entirely because it has nothing to do with oversleeping, loving pleasure etc. It's a terrible phenomenon that affects large groups of people like in nations, communities, provinces etc.

It's a curse that needs divine intervention to be overcome.

15 BASIC BIBLICAL KEYS TO POVERTY

Question:
What can a Christian do to avoid this?

Answer:
The very first thing a Christian can do is to recognize it for what it is and cry to God for help. It's usually spiritual and only God can change times and seasons (Daniel 2: 20-21).

But before scarcity ever strikes, which will be something like economic recessions and depressions in our own time, a Christian should actually plan for its likelihood of occurrence like Joseph did in Genesis 41:34-36. He made the nation of Egypt save 20% of all their proceeds for seven years in preparation for the famine. And as a result, he did not only save Egypt from the peril of the famine, but also the world at large during his time. Start saving certain portions of your income now so as to be ready when economic downturn strikes. Don't consume everything. That's what connects one to poverty during famine season.

In addition to this, a Christian must stay close

to God for specific instructions. He says in Psalm 32:8 that He will instruct you, teach you the way you shall go and guide you with His eyes. His instruction at such times is your life-boat to escape the scourge. For instance, in Genesis 26:1-4 He told Isaac where to go and what to do right in the midst of the famine; and instead of Isaac becoming poor during that season, he actually became so prosperous that even an entire nation envied him (Genesis 26:12-16). Don't joke with divine instructions. Your life seriously depends on it.

Conclusion

So far, the Lord has revealed some biblical causes of poverty to us. The purpose is not just to know, document or preach them, rather they were revealed so that we can avoid them and be free from poverty.

According to John 8:32, only the truth that is known sets free. So, go through these causes one by one and if any of them is still in your life, quickly get rid of them.

-Uncontrolled Sleep
-Oppressing the Poor
-Showering Gifts on the Rich
-Idle Chatter
-Withholding More Than is Right
-Laziness
-Making Yourself Rich
-Disdaining Correction

- Loving Pleasure
- Borrowing
- Drunkenness/Gluttony
- Hasty Plans
- Following Frivolity
- Hastening After Riches
- Dwelling in Famine

Now what?
Flee from all of these and POVERTY will leave you alone.
Jesus said in John 13:17(NLT) - "You know these things- now do them! That is the path of blessing."

May the Lord connect you and your entire household to His unending source of Financial Blessings in Jesus Name!

WHY YOU REALLY NEED JESUS!

You might have heard a lot of Preachers talk about the importance of surrendering one's life to Jesus and even the dangers of not doing so at one time or the other without you being really moved. But with these three (3) important reasons highlighted below, I strongly believe you will not need another sermon before deciding to yield to His saving grace regardless of your religious beliefs.

1. **You have an Enemy to overcome:** There is an adversary who is all out to steal from you, kill you and destroy you regardless of your level of education, moral uprightness, societal influence or even religious beliefs. He is Devil by name (John 10:10, 1 Peter 5: 8), and he doesn't release any of

his captives until he completely destroys their souls in hell. The ONLY One Who can deliver you from his manipulations and also save your soul from him is Jesus Christ.

2. **You have an Appointment to keep:** Being alive and reading this implies you have a very important and inevitable appointment to keep. It is an appointment with death (Hebrews 9:27). Death is the sure end of all mortals (of which you are part); and to enable you prepare for this appointment without fear of eternal damnation, you need Jesus. He is the ONLY One Who has power over death (Revelation 1:18).

3. **You have a Judge to face:** Upon departure from this earth, you will have to stand before a judgment throne to render an account of your earthly life (Hebrews 9:27, Romans 14:12). The outcome of this judgment is what will determine your eternal abode which will either be Heaven

15 BASIC BIBLICAL KEYS TO POVERTY

or the Lake of fire. Interestingly, the Judge Who will preside over your case and also decide where you will spend your eternity is Jesus (John 5:21-30, 2 Timothy 4:1). I perceive you are thinking "is God not our Judge? Why Jesus?' Well, you are not wrong. But God the Father Himself is the One Who handed over all the judgment to His Son, Jesus Christ. Read the verse 22 of that John chapter 5. So Jesus is the ONLY One Who has the power to either judge you guilty or guiltless in eternity.

Now that you know these, the wisest thing you can do for yourself is to quickly establish a relationship with Jesus, since you don't even know how close your appointment with death is. To do this, say this prayer aloud:

"Lord Jesus, I am a sinner and I cannot help myself. Wash me in your precious blood and make me a new creature. I open the door of my heart to you today, come into my life and become my Lord and Savior. Grant me the grace to overcome the devil, prepare me for eternity

and help me to escape the judgment reserved for sinners. Thank You Jesus for saving me. Amen."

Congratulations! You are now SAVED. Go and sin no more.

To learn more about your new relationship with Jesus, kindly send an Email to info@gloem.org or emancipation4souls@yahoo.com, we will send you a material that will help you. You can also call, text or send whatsapp message to +1 587 9735910 or +1 587 9695910 for further assistance.

And to learn more about God, His Word and His plans for your life, kindly visit our Facebook page [*https://www.facebook.com/gloem.org*] for daily meditation in the Word of God (all year round) and our Blog page [*https://gloem.org/my-blog*] for life transforming publications.

You are also invited to listen to Freedom Podcast: The Official Weekly Podcast of Global Emancipation Ministries – Calgary via https://anchor.fm/gloem

All these great resources capable of developing your spiritual stamina will help you become an overcomer in life regardless of what comes your way.

PRAYER POINTS

1. Father, thank You for opening my eyes to the truths contained in this book.
2. Father, please cause everything attracting poverty into my life to be destroyed.
3. I cancel everything contrary to my prosperity in Jesus' Name.
4. God of all possibilities, please cause my grass to become green again.
5. From today, my financial breakthrough shall no longer be delayed in Jesus' Name.
6. Father, beginning from now, please release upon me and my household the ability to get wealth in the Name of Jesus.
7. Father, I thank You for answering all my prayers. Glory be to Your Holy Name. Hallelujah!

BECOME A FINANCIAL PARTNER WITH JESUS

At ***Global Emancipation Ministries - Calgary***, our mandate is ***to liberate men through the knowledge of the Truth*** and our mission statement is ***creating channels through which men can encounter the Truth - [Isaiah 61:1-3; John 8:32, 36; I Thessalonians 5:24].***

Our Ministerial Activities include Rural and Urban Evangelical Outreaches, Prison Evangelism, Hospital Ministrations, Mobilization for Missions Support, Teaching of the undiluted Word of God, Scripture-Based Seminars, Discipleship, Training of Field Missionaries and Empowerment of underprivileged ones among other Field Ministerial Tasks.

If you sense the Lord is calling you to reach out to the lost by engaging in any of these activities or by assisting those involved with your resources, please feel free to join us. Let us come together as we take the Gospel of our Lord Jesus Christ to the hurting and forgotten ones. [Mark 16:15-20].

Please join us in these kingdom projects by making your weekly, monthly, quarterly or annual donations to Global Emancipation Ministries – Calgary.

You can visit the "GIVE" section on our website, www.gloem.org, to learn about the ways to give.

-

For acknowledgement, please advise your donations to us by email: info@gloem.org or emancipation4souls@yahoo.com, and kindly include your details i.e. name, address, email and location. Alternatively, you can simply call +1 587 9735910 to do same.

You can also volunteer your gifts and talents

in the service of the Lord through our ministerial platforms regardless of your location. To get information on how to go about this, please visit www.gloem.org and contact us via email: info@gloem.org or emancipation4souls@yahoo.com.

God bless you.

About the Author

By the special grace of God, **Anthony O. Adefarakan** is the privileged President of **Global Emancipation Ministries - Calgary (GLOEM)** with headquarters in Canada, North America and **Emancipating Truth Ministry International (ETMI)** with headquarters in Nigeria, West Africa.

The Lord called him into the field ministry in February 2008 with the mandate to liberate men through the knowledge of the Truth, and by December 2012 he was ordained and commissioned as the Pioneer Pastor – in – Charge of The Redeemed Christian Church of God, Revelation Parish, Shalom Area under Delta Province III, Nigeria where he served until 1st February 2015 when he officially handed over to a new Pastor in order to focus on his field ministry to which the Lord had earlier called him and for which the authority of the church had already prayed and released him to undertake.

On 29th September 2013, he was awarded a Post Graduate Diploma in Tent – Making Mission from the Redeemed Christian School of Missions, Nigeria (RECSOM, Asaba Campus) where he also had the privilege to train Pastors and Missionaries as a lecturer in 2017.

Since the commissioning of his field ministry in 2015 he has had the opportunity to lead his ministry officers to field ministrations in different Prisons, Hospitals, Orphanages, Rural communities, Camp settlements, Markets, Local churches among other places with great successes on all occasions – such as salvation of sinners, healing of the sick, financial empowerment of mission churches, provision of relief materials to the poor, provision of medical services to the underprivileged, baptism in the Holy Ghost, deliverance from demonic oppression, release of inmates just to mention a few - all to the glory of God Who alone is the Doer.

He is the author of other best-selling titles such as ***The Law of Kinds, Learning From the Ants, The Immutability of God's Counsel, Surely there is an End, Life Applicable lessons from the Book of Ruth, One thing is Needful Weekly Devotional Guide, Life Applicable Revelations from God's Word*** **(Volumes 1 and 2)** among others.

He is blissfully married to Ifeoluwa A. Adefarakan and their marriage is fruitful to the glory of God.

Jesus is his Message, Freedom is the Outcome!

Isaiah 61:1-3

www.ingramcontent.com/pod-product-compliance
Lightning Source LLC
Chambersburg PA
CBHW060412080526
44583CB00012B/537